JUST SAY YES,
AND GO!

by Ed Rudolphi

It was the same invitation she'd extended several different times before.

With a pearly-white smile plastered on her face and enthusiasm in her voice, she proved my prediction to be correct by saying the words:

"Hey, Eddie! You comin' on the next missions' trip to El Salvador?"

At that point, I had shrugged off her offer so many times, I couldn't believe she hadn't relented. I had made every excuse, dodged every loophole, and shut every door on the possibility of my attendance. But, because I knew she wouldn't stop mentioning the trip until I caved, that morning I finally—and begrudgingly—gave her my yes.

Anything to get you off my case, I thought to myself.

Little did I know that my acceptance of her invitation would lead to the many stories I am writing about today. From the number of lives that have been transformed; relationships that have been cultivated; sick bodies that have been restored back to health, to the many lost souls found, my decision to fly to a country I knew little about for a trip I was in no way enthusiastic about attending changed

13

the trajectory of my life and that of many others' as well. But, after traveling there and back, completing missions for over 20 years now, I often imagine what it would be like if I hadn't given Nancy my yes. I wonder what kind of words I would be writing today if I had continued to avoid her after church in order to decline her request. There would be miracles I would not have witnessed, world-changing people I would not have met. Doors would still remain closed, and lives would not have been transformed. It's a scary thought to explore—a heartbreaking reality I never want to live—which is why I'm most thankful for Nancy's invitation and the Holy Spirit in me urging me to cave.

But, while I will never have to go on wondering what would've happened if I said no, my heart *does* break wondering about the many others who *are* saying no— followers of Jesus Christ who feel like missionary work doesn't concern them; believers who are hesitant to step out of their comfort zone and serve. The thought of it troubles me, and quite frankly makes my stomach turn, because I have seen the other side of my decision to get uncomfortable. I have seen the impact of leaving the confines of what I'm familiar with and serving a region I wouldn't usually make space for. For me, that was saying yes to a mission's trip to El Salvador.

For you? Well, that's what you are on track to find out.

In Mark 16:15 NIV, Jesus shares some of His most famous departing words to His disciples before He ascended to be at the right hand of the Father. He says:

"...Go into all the world and preach the Good News to everyone."

Notice how Jesus didn't say, "Go wherever you feel comfortable." Instead, He commissioned those who follow Him to go out into *all the world*.

So, the question becomes: What parts of the world are currently left unchanged by the power of the gospel? And, most importantly, what is the corner of the world that God is calling you to?

Is it the downtown city streets of your community?

Is it that classmate who sits all by himself at your lunch table?

Are you called to minister to the cashier who rings you out every day at your local grocery store?

Are you to go to the bar down the road to preach the gospel?

Are you commissioned to go and preach in a completely different continent?

What is the corner of the world God is calling you to? And, how can your contribution change it?

Not sure? Well, I'm writing this book to tell you one thing:

You'll never know until you say yes.

My name is Ed Rudolphi, a friend of God and a missionary to the great country of El Salvador. While I've been on many missions' trips to other countries before my visit, Holy Spirit made it clear that El Salvador was the corner of the world He was calling me to. Born again in the year 1986, I had no idea that God could use someone like me in a country thousands of miles away. I didn't know that when I said "yes" to Jesus, I was also saying yes to Mark

16:15. And, when I gave my "yes" to Nancy Ashman, the Holy Spirit in me only reminded me about my original yes to Jesus. And, because Nancy's invitation reaffirmed my calling, I now want this book to reaffirm yours too.

Mark 16:15 wasn't just an exclusive invitation for Peter, James, John and the other eight disciples who were present that day. No, His command was for the eleven disciples present that day *and* for every disciple to follow after. Therefore, if you are a follower of Jesus, the invitation to go out into all the world and preach the Good News is extended to you as well. And, like a Nancy Ashman, this book is your reminder. With ten awe-inspiring stories of men and women who dared to say yes to the call, men and women whom I would've never met if *I* hadn't said yes, consider the content of these pages to be what Nancy was to me: a persistent, never-ending, almost nagging invitation to obey the Master's commission—to go out into all the world and preach the good news. You don't need to be a picture-perfect Christian to be used by God. If you study the lives of Jesus' twelve disciples and know my story as well, you will see that God loves to use imperfect people. He called them before time even began. Ephesians 1:4 says so. What makes you think He's changed His mind?

So, even while you may be starting off this book hesitant of the importance of obeying Mark 16:15, not to mention how He can use your obedience to change lives, my prayer is that you would finish this book with a deep conviction about our Master's commission. I pray that your heart is pricked with the reality of what obeying the still small voice of Holy Spirit can do with every testimony you read. There are lives out there that need to be changed, people who need to be served, a gospel that needs to be preached. And, whether you believe it or not, the chance to make an impact outside of your comfort zone is available to you. So, what are you waiting for? Let this book encourage you to do what you're called to do, go where you're assigned to go, and obey the Master's Great Commission—winning souls for Jesus.

CHAPTER ONE
LIDIA

I will always remember that first moment we landed in El Salvador—the warmth brought on by the sun, the buzz from the other church members I traveled with, the nagging thought I had wrestled with the entire plane ride there:

What exactly am I getting myself into?

All I knew was that I was there to serve, as I had done before on other missions' trips, but I was not prepared to be welcomed by such an incredible group of people.

It wasn't long after we arrived that we were met with the team from El Salvador—the one we were called to serve alongside. I was one of the newest members on the trip, so I could not join in on what seemed like a reunion between the citizens from El Salvador and a handful of my church family. But, after being introduced to so many new faces, that was the day I met two people who—while I didn't know it at the time—would play such a large role in my story: Loidy and Lidia.

Allow me to introduce the two.

Both Loidy and Lidia at the time of our meeting were Ultima Harvest Commission leaders assigned to my church family's team for construction. I realized right off the bat that Loidy was outgoing and a very hard worker, and I count her as one of the most memorable leaders I was privileged to serve alongside. But, if there was one person whom I can describe as the bridge that connected me with the other missionaries soon to be mentioned in this book, it would be Lidia—Lidia Zelaya Rivas.

When I first met Lidia, she was incredibly quiet. She said little, but led well and worked with extreme vibrancy. Even though our communication was fractured due to the language barrier between my fluent English and her fluent Spanish, there was a light that undeniably shone bright within her, and her work in Castillo Del Rey bore sweet fruit. A couple of surface-level "¡Hola's!" and "¿Cómo estás?" later, my church family and I got to work. We came for the sole purpose of ministering to the citizens of El Salvador by building a church and constructing other projects. However, in the same way we came to minister, I had no idea that the people in El Salvador would ultimately minister to us. And, so it was the case for me and my soon-to-be friendship with Lidia.

I didn't learn of Lidia's story all at once. It took several trips back, many phone calls, and emails for me to stay in contact with Lidia long enough for me to learn her testimony. But, as our friendship was being built, I wanted to know where the light within her came from. I became curious about the origins of her hard work and strong leadership skills. Sure enough, as the years passed, I learned what her story was—how her trials, obstacles, and hardships shaped her into the woman she is today.

This is what I learned:

At age fourteen, Lidia dedicated her life to Jesus with the same ministry she was leading on the day I met her. (Talk about a moment coming full circle!) However, while her faith as a fourteen-year-old carried her in adolescence, she encountered many painful bumps along the way.

Persecution is what our Savior, Jesus Christ, promises to those who follow Him. And, while many of us don't expect to face that persecution at a young age, this was the case for Lidia. But, though she endured much abuse and suffering, Lidia never stopped following Jesus. That's what struck me the most about her story. Even at a young age enduring the storms of life, she never once turned her back on her faith. What she had encountered at the age of fourteen was real, and she wouldn't let anyone convince her otherwise.

Not only that, but Lidia also had a strong desire to lead more people to Jesus. The freedom she experienced in His presence urged her to tell as many people as she could about Him. In fact, her list of people began with one living in her very own home:

Her father.

She prayed for her father's salvation constantly—always believed that one day his soul might be saved.

"The pursuit of Christ is constant," she told me once, "no matter when we think He's going to answer us."

Therefore, she held onto and studied Matthew 7:7 NIV to remind herself of how she must stay persistent in prayer concerning her father. The Scripture is as follows:

"Ask and it will be given to you; seek and you will find; knock and the door will be opened to you."

These were the words of Jesus.

The closer we became, the more she requested I pray for his salvation too. Many times, we would pray together. Along with Matthew 7:7, I would encourage her to never give up, to never stop believing for her father's salvation. Therefore, we prayed about him for years. In many ways, the support I was able to give her through prayer and encouragement made an impact on our long history of friendship. But, even though our prayer meetings wouldn't begin until years after our initial greeting in 2002, a need in her community arose within the first week of my being there.

There was a car accident—a brutal one—an accident that took the lives of two young adults and severely injured several others, many of whom were scheduled to go on a missions' trip with Lidia's church later in the year. And, as the community mourned and grieved over the shocking tragedy, the question of whether or not the church was able to go to Baja Verapaz, Guatemala to complete missions became a part of the conversation. Finances were tight, and the amount needed could no longer be collected due to the tragedy. And, while God could've used anything and anyone to meet their need, I was thankful that He called my church and me to be in El Salvador at that specific time—to use us. We prayed with Lidia and her team. We mourned over the lives lost with them. And, then we were able to demonstrate the love of God through our financial support.

My church paid the amount that was owed in order for Lidia and her church family to attend their trip to Guatemala. Their joy was rewarding. Their tears and celebration were humbling. And, it wasn't until later when I would begin thinking about what the outcome might have been if my church and I weren't there to serve. Sure, God could use anyone and anything to reach His children's needs, as He promises us in Philippians 4:19. But, the fact that God wanted and chose to use *us* to serve and meet the needs of those grieving in El Salvador speaks volumes. Imagine if we wouldn't have gone. Imagine if I, myself, had said no to attending this mission's trip. I would've missed out on one of the greatest opportunities to demonstrate the love and care of God.

What about you? What opportunities could you be missing by staying in your comfort zone, only saying yes to what's familiar? Don't you think if God could use my church family and me to meet a need, He could use you too? Think about what's stopping you from going into the corner of the world He's called you to go. Is it fear? Insecurity? Doubt? Whatever it is, bring it to the Lord and ask Him to help you through it. You may have a Lidia you're assigned to who's waiting for you to say, 'Yes.' There might be a need God wants to meet through you, but your fear is stopping you from going all in.

Not only that, but there could be a God-ordained friendship waiting for you on the other side of your obedience. This was true for Lidia and me. While we were first connected in 2002, our next conversation wouldn't be had until the year 2004 when my church family and I revisited El Salvador for missions. I made it a point to ask about her again, and when we reunited, she couldn't believe I had remembered her! On the contrary, I couldn't believe she'd thought I'd forget. Her warmth and strong leadership skills left an impression on us all, and I was excited to work with her once again. What I didn't know is that our time of working together in El Salvador wouldn't be forever, as I soon learned that Lidia was called to complete missions in Cambodia.

The year was 2010 when both Loidy and Lidia set out to Cambodia for the first time together. With their faith in God alone, they followed His call on their lives traveling miles away from their home, and therefore, preventing me from seeing them for quite some time.

Our good-bye was heartfelt. At that point of our friendship, we had learned each other's testimonies, became close with each other's family and friends, made frequent phone calls, shared Scripture verses, and encouraged one another in the Word. Lidia and I continued to pray for her father's salvation as well. Therefore, saying good-bye was difficult—especially because we were both unsure if we'd ever serve alongside one another again. We hugged. We cried. We promised we'd keep in contact however we could—through Facebook, writing letters, whatever it took. And, though it was bittersweet traveling back to El Salvador again the year after without being able to see her, I knew that she was doing everything the Lord told her to do with the same excellence I saw in her when we first met.

The year 2016 proved me right.

All the while Lidia and I were unsure of whether or not we'd serve with one another again, God already knew how He was going to use our connection for His glory. By the time 2016 rolled around, He already gave Lidia a vision of what to build in Cambodia. She began envisioning a church and schoolhouse to replace the existing empty lot she originally saw before her. After feeling that familiar tug from Holy Spirit, our church family felt an urge to donate $30,000 to Lidia's vision—a donation that would help build the church and school, and later, apartments. The building was completed in 2019, and Lidia's dedication, commitment, and passion for what God was doing in Cambodia is still alive today. Not only that, but all of the prayers Lidia and I prayed concerning her father's salvation came to fruition as Lidia sat beside him on his last day on earth, watching him take his final breaths. All of Lidia's prayers for her father came true right before he passed. He gave his heart to God.

It was his salvation that reminded me of why missionary work is so important.

It's not just about supporting a ministry financially. It's ultimately about supporting a ministry through prayer, encouragement, and friendship. And, hearing Lidia rejoice over her father's, "Yes," to the Lord was the most rewarding phone call of my life. On top of that, knowing that my small participation in serving a community far from home by providing education, shelter, hospitality, and truth through the power of the gospel is incredibly heart-warming.

And, it all came from one simple, "Yes," to Nancy.

I wonder what your "yes" to going out into all the world could do too.

JOURNAL IT

Ask Holy Spirit to show you some reasons why you haven't said, "Yes," yet and journal those reasons here. Then, pray that God will help you remove the barrier.

_____

_____

_____

_____

_____

_____

_____

_____

_____

_____

_____

_____

_____

_____

Through the many years of knowing and building a friendship with Lidia, she has connected me to many other missionaries along the way. Soon after my original meeting with her in 2002, the Lord used her to introduce me to another incredible world-changer—a leader whom I had the honor of meeting all the way back in 2004:

Her name is Marcela.

CHAPTER TWO

MARCELA

Part of the role Lidia played at Ultima Harvest Commission (the ministry in El Salvador that my church partnered with) was to lead, train, and teach other ministry students as well. Two of these students were Ilsia and

Marcela. I met both of them in the year 2004—each of them having their own unique story that I am eager to tell you about as you continue to turn the pages. However, I worked closely with Marcela during my second trip to El Salvador for one week doing construction.

Unbeknownst to me, one week of working together would turn into years of friendship. Even more—family.

The significance of her leadership was very clear from the moment I met her. Marcela was older than her other classmates in Master's Commission. She was twenty-two, whereas the others were around the ages of eighteen and nineteen. I often called her "Mother Hen" once I realized the age difference. However, it wasn't just her age that earned Marcela the title. It was also the way her classmates used to go to her in a time of need, requesting for her advice, and esteeming her words more highly than they would have from other students. The role she played in her classmates' lives revealed that there was a special call on her life. She was a sister everyone could trust—a good friend and a mother figure for many. And, after having learned of her good character during my second stay in El

Salvador, the Holy Spirit opened up an opportunity towards the end of my trip, showing me how I could contribute to the corner of the world He's assigned to me.

He revealed this:

Marcela had a need.

At the end of each missions' trip, when we—— Americans—are scheduled to leave El Salvador to travel back home, our friends in El Salvador are always kind enough to throw us what they call a *despedida*—which is essentially a going-away party for their new American friends. They feel it is the only proper way to send us off with well wishes and many blessings. My recent experiences with *despedidas* have been extremely special. They'll clothe the ladies in beautiful dresses that are inspired by their culture, and the guys will wear cowboy hats. They'll dance to music, sing songs, eat great food, and celebrate vibrantly with the whole missionary team. And, while each of these celebrations have been significant to me, I still remember the party we had in 2004—the last night of my second missions' trip there. Every *despedida* provides an opportunity to sponsor a student we met there during our time of ministry. And, even though it was only my second visit, I knew I wanted to sponsor Marcela and another student I met at the time. Part of this is because of how impacted I was to hear about what a sponsorship did for another student. A friend of mine had pledged to give $25 a month to a student back when he first began mission work in 1999 in El Salvador. His sponsorship alone turned into the investment of five churches built in Panama through the work of the student he sponsored! Not to mention, my friend's belief in her created a God-ordained friendship and other divine opportunities as well.

Moved by the testimony, I too filled out a card, pledging to give $50 a month to both Marcela and the other student each. However, I later learned that the other student—while still pursuing the Lord—was no longer in ministry. Therefore, the $50 a month I pledged to her went to Marcela instead, allowing me to sponsor Marcela for a full $100 a month.

I didn't know what would come of my offering at the time. I just knew to obey. And, just as with every moment of obedience, there came the opportunity for something greater. In Marcela's case, it was redemption. My sponsorship created such a bond between Marcela and my wife and I that I had the privilege of hearing just a small piece of her story. Growing up in a household with her mother and brothers, Marcela did not have a clear picture of what a healthy marriage looks like. While she and her brothers all shared the same mom, they all had different fathers. Her mother lived a rough life and brought many different men into the home during Marcela's childhood. To this day, I could only imagine how that impacted her as just a young girl.

But, Marcela was set apart, and she was serious about walking with the Lord all the way into ministry school at King's Castle in El Salvador. My obedience, while I didn't know it at the time, would be used as a bridge to redeem her story.

My sponsorship supported her all the way up until her wedding day—the first wedding her whole family has ever had.Marcela's milestone, being the first to be married in her family, was the redemption she needed after growing up without that example. Marcela broke a generational curse when she said, "I do," to her now-husband, Efren. The ministry work they do together as a family in Romania, now with two children—Valeria and Josias—is groundbreaking. Who knew that one gift could lead to a broken generational curse? One act of obedience could lead to a monumental moment for someone's family?

And, now I ask you: Is there something you have that you could give to your corner of the world? Do you have a financial gift? Or, prayer to offer? What about love? How can you give that to make a difference?

You never know what your giving—in any form—can do. Take some time to journal some things you are sensing Holy Spirit asking you to lend:

_____

_____

_____

_____

_____

_____

_____

_____

_____

_____

_____

_____

_____

The Lord opened up many doors for Marcela, and He blessed my wife and me, allowing us to stay in contact with her throughout the years. Throughout those many years of our friendship, Marcela has visited our home here in the United States many times. Our work done together in the year 2004 and then again on my third trip back in 2005 led to even more connections made with other students in her class, including one of her classmates named Eric, whom I wouldn't see again until the year 2014. But, the next student who served a large purpose in my missionary journey is a student that Lidia also connected me to in the year of 2004. Having no clue what this next person would mean to me down the road, I was introduced to someone I will never forget—Ilsia.

CHAPTER THREE

ILSIA

Many statistics will tell you that those who grow up in a faith-based environment abandon the church when they get older. Some statistics will even show how unlikely it is for a child to grow in their faith if they did not grow up in a religious environment. However, this was not the case for Ilsia. Ilsia grew up in a home that was non-Christian, and therefore, learned concepts that were far from biblical teaching.

Yet, if you met Ilsia, you would never know it.

Ilsia's faith was one of the first things I noticed about her when we first met. She didn't have to say much. Her trust in God spoke for itself. I met her alongside Marcela in 2004, but unlike Marcella, I wasn't able to see her in the year 2005. Ilsia had committed the next year of her life ministering to those in Equatorial Guinea in Africa and was scheduled to return the year after.

However, when 2006 rolled around, an unfortunate series of events prevented her homecoming.

Ilsia, as well as the other students who traveled to Africa with her, were diagnosed with an extreme illness— malaria. I hadn't known much about her then, but I remember having deep concern for her and the other familiar faces I was only recently getting to know. My fear was that I would not see them again.

This realization was a turning point in my journey of becoming a missionary.

Thanks be to God, their malaria diagnosis did not tell the rest of the story. The students recovered and were able to return home. While I wasn't there to welcome them back, as I did not visit El Salvador in the year 2007, Ilsia and I reunited in the year 2008. This fifth visit back to their country was significant for many reasons. Much of my heart and passion for El Salvador came from this visit, in fact. From the church members I traveled with (becoming more like family, at this point) to the new people I met as we constructed new projects, traveling to El Salvador in 2008 created a plethora of special memories. Much of it had to do with Ilsia.

At this point of my faith journey, I had been saved for twenty-two years. My relationship with the Holy Spirit was personal and authentic, and I was thankful to have known plenty of other believers who had deep walks with the Lord as well. However, throughout all of my twenty-two years of salvation, I never had anyone call me a spiritual father. I myself had plenty, but no one had ever told me that they considered me theirs. I understood that a spiritual father is one who mentors, disciples, teaches, and loves their spiritual children as if they were their own. I had become thankful for the spiritual leaders in my life and how they had helped me grow and learn more about the heart of Christ. Therefore, to carry the title of spiritual father was not something I would ever take lightly. This is exactly why I was shocked to hear that in the year 2008—after giving advice to Ilsia, per her request—she would later consider me to be her spiritual father.

Our conversation leading up to her decision went a little something like this:

She had come up to me sheepishly in the middle of working on our project. I could tell that she had something on her mind. I soon learned that her concerned expression involved a man that she was interested in. He had a great job, was from the states, and wanted to marry Ilsia, moving her to the United States as well. The only problem—what Ilsia was concerned about—is that Ilsia had a vision to move to India, continuing missionary work. She had dreamed of it for a great deal of time and hadn't entertained any other future until she met this gentleman, who did not share the same heart as she did for the mission field. The thought of abandoning her dream, and ultimately her calling, troubled her—especially because it would be for the sake of an eternal covenant, a marriage that didn't align with her missionary work. I could tell that Ilsia was looking for sound advice, as this was no small decision to make. She trusted me to be the one to give it to her. Therefore, I asked her a question that I didn't know would mean as much as it did until she told me later.

"You love him," I told her, "and he loves you. But, does he love the mission field the way you do? Does he love it enough to support your vision?"

I then proceeded to share verses like Jeremiah 1:5 NIV, which says: "Before I formed you in the womb I knew you, before you were born I set you apart; I appointed you as a prophet to the nations.", explaining that God had a plan for her life before she was even born. I also shared 2 Corinthians 6:14-15 NIV, which says:

Do not be yoked together with unbelievers. For what do righteousness and wickedness have in common? Or what fellowship can light have with darkness? What harmony is there between Christ and Belial? Or what does a believer have in common with an unbeliever?

Evidently, the words I shared with her that day were the exact words Ilsia needed to hear in order to come up with her conclusion. She knew what she needed to do after our conversation. She ended the relationship, left the gentleman with well wishes, and decided to wait for the one who had a similar dream as hers. Not only that, but out of the advice that I was happy to give her, my role as advisor in her life went to a deeper level. From that point on, she began to call me her spiritual father.

It was a title I was not expecting to be given at all, but that moment alone began to heighten how important missionary work was. It wasn't just a matter of traveling between nations. Instead, my work as a missionary meant making an impact in people's stories, making a difference, changing hearts and lives…all because I was obedient to the call on my life.

And, I believe that there are many more Ilsia's out there—Ilsia's in your corner of the world who are waiting for you to say yes.

Thereare people who need to hear the words God has given you to speak. They need your voice to be encouraged, strengthened, challenged, and convicted. Not only that, but you may need their voice, their faith, and their testimony to further your walk with the Lord, too.

I came to this conclusion once I began realizing that Ilsia was ministering to me at the same time I was ministering to her.

I will never forget one of my favorite moments where she poured into me—though she didn't know it at the time. I did not have the chance of realizing how little I took for granted until I was touched by her story. Due to my previous complacency, I didn't know how often I missed out on the opportunity to give thanks to God for moments I've experienced that others haven't. Ilsia taught me to never take life for granted. What I consider to be normal may not be normal to someone else. For example, I will never forget the tears in Ilsia's eyes when I purchased a birthday cake to celebrate her during one of my many visits. What I thought was a simple act of courtesy to buy a cake for her birthday turned into a significant revelation for me. Ilsia was overjoyed by the notion because she never had anyone buy a cake for her birthday before. Something that was so common to me was extraordinary for her. How eye-opening! Not to mention, I also remember being able to celebrate alongside Ilsia when she led her father, Rafael, to the Lord right before he passed. That moment ministered to me like no other—a moment I could've missed if I would've said no.

JOURNAL IT

Think about those who have ministered to you in the past. How have they impacted your life?

_____

_____

_____

_____

_____

_____

Now, think about those who you know you are called to minister to. It may or may not be someone from across the world. You may be called to speak to the people you see every day. Ask Holy Spirit what you should say to them. Ask Him what they need to hear. And, not only that, but tell Him that you're open to Him using whoever He wants to speak into your life. You may be on the brink of receiving an awesome revelation. Ask Him to help you to keep your heart and mind open to the lessons you could learn from those He's assigned to you.

_____

_____

_____

_____

_____

_____

_____

_____

I'm here to testify that saying the words God puts on your heart can change someone's life forever. In Ilsia's case, my conversation with her led her to make a crucial decision. As hard as it might've been for her to leave the gentleman behind, she continued to wait and be patient for the man God had for her. Our conversation gave her faith to believe she would get married to a man who shared her dream—a man who had the same heart for the Lord in the same region for the same purpose. Low and behold, God was faithful in response to Ilsia's patience. He brought along the perfect man for her in the year of 2011—Daniel.

Daniel also had a heart to minister to the region of India. They got married shortly after raising funds together and soon left the camp Ilsia worked at in El Salvador to go to India in 2014. When I went to visit them in India in 2016, I was encouraged to know that their hearts for the Lord were still steadfast. The same faith I saw in Ilsia when I first met her was the same faith I saw during my visit. In fact, her faith was even stronger. They were living in a small house with a dirt floor, but their gratitude far exceeded the circumstance. (This was another learning moment for me. Similar to Ilsia's excitement over a birthday cake, I was also humbled by their contentment with their living conditions. What was normal for them wasn't normal for me. This taught me once again to never take things for granted.) They knew that they were called to do missions, and they wouldn't let anything stop them. Even when the year 2017 rolled around, they were still faithful to their call. They had to move out of India to Cambodia since the Hindu population began to express deep hatred for Christians. Their house was searched, and wanting to remain firm in their mission, they told the officers that they were there to learn English. But, their efforts did not hold, as they eventually had to leave the region. Even still, Daniel and Ilsia remained faithful.

Ilsia underwent an extreme illness in the year of 2021. Her sickness was life-threatening, so much so that she was told she could not go back into the mission fields. When I contacted Daniel and Ilsia to share in their grief, I was blown away by Ilsia's response:

"We're missionaries," she told me. "We don't need a lot. It doesn't matter if we have a house or a car. We're still going to go to the mission field."

And, it is through her life and through her faith that I too will continue to go out into the mission field—into all the world—no matter what challenges I face.

Will you?

CHAPTER FOUR

MARISOL

The year 2008 was the year that changed El Salvador for me. After that year, I didn't want to leave. I made the decision to visit as many times as possible—with my church, and eventually, on my own accord. And, through these years, I've met incredible sets of missionaries like Lidia, Marcella, and at that point, Ilsia. In fact, you'll soon realize how each missionary mentioned makes up a long thread of intertwined friendships, connections, and new introductions. Each person I met was a result of meeting someone mutual, which created a beautiful community of each missionary building up and helping one another. An example of this could easily be pulled from Ilsia's story. When I purchased that cake for Ilsia, I was not the only one who helped make that possible. Two women, a part of the long thread of missionary friendships, were on board. One is named Jocelyn, who I am greatly anticipating introducing you to in a later chapter. The other woman, however, is another significant person I connected with in my journey. Her name is Marisol, and like the others, she has become like family.

The year 2009 was a quiet one. It was a year when I didn't travel to El Salvador, which—having found amazing family in that country—was painful for me to wait another year. This is why I had every intention of making the year 2010 count, revisiting the friends I had made in El Salvador, making new ones, and getting closer with my church family in the meantime. I knew that my sixth visit here would be special when I met Marisol—a quiet, intelligent leader with whom I was connected through Lidia and Ilsia. We didn't talk that much because we couldn't understand one another's language, but we communicated with warm smiles and friendly expressions. Her life before we met intrigued me once I was able to hear about it. Having been born the same year I received Jesus as my Lord and Savior was one of the many things that connected us. However, once I found out about her life growing up, the many degrees she's studied for and achieved, and her clear call to ministry, I realized that there was a depth to Marisol that made her good deeds shine incredibly bright.

Her story is as follows:

Marisol was born to two Christian parents named Lorenzo and Sonia on January 5th, 1986 in Guatemala City, Guatemala. She grew up with a great example of what it looks like to love God from her parents. At nine years old, Marisol made her faith personal and accepted Jesus into her heart, learning about God in Sunday school from that point on. Even further, she even became a Sunday school teacher at the age of twelve! As she continued to grow in her walk with her Lord, her teen years would cause her to make strong decisions about her life and her relationship with Jesus.

Though she had a great example of what it looked like to follow Jesus from her parents growing up, her life at home changed drastically when her brothers became extremely ill. The devastating news led to her mother following Jesus even more passionately, but her father's path began to look different. As Marisol's father was a professing Christian in her youth, he soon turned away from God and denounced his faith. The severity of his decision was revealed once he began to forbid Marisol's mother from attending church as well, justifying that it was for the sake of the family. Though congregating with her church family was prevented, her mother never turned away from God, and between her mother's strong faith and Marisol's Sunday school classes teaching her to seek the Lord, Marisol never turned from God either.

Her pursuit after the Lord resulted in her crossing paths with the same ministry my church would partner with in El Salvador, leading Marisol and I to meet in the year 2010. Two years after I met her, I returned to the church in El Salvador and asked if she was present. When they told me she wasn't, I was quite disappointed—certain that I might not ever see her again. However, just as I was getting ready to board the bus, I was astonished to hear a voice calling my name.

It was Marisol!

What are the odds?

I couldn't believe she had remembered me! Then, on another occasion, needing more materials to run the camp we were working in, Marisol and I accidentally ran into each other in town. But, these seemingly happy coincidences (which were really, undoubtedly God's doing) weren't the moments that significantly connected us. Instead, it was what I learned during the time she and I shared together—a time where I realized just how powerful Marisol's decision to take part in full-time ministry was. Marisol was especially intelligent—attaining degrees I didn't even know existed. From graduating as a Vocational Technician Accountant in 2004 from the National General Francisco Menendez Institute to entering the National University of San Salvador with a degree in International Marketing to working in Commercial *Exportadora*, I couldn't believe all that she had achieved. Not only that, but her many academic accomplishments made me wonder how she found herself in full-time ministry. She could've been a full-time international accountant—a successful businesswoman! But, she chose ministry instead? Why would she choose that?

Her answer blew me away.

After she and I had met and completed missions together in El Salvador, she later told me that she was deeply inspired by the missionary work I had completed, along with the number of missionaries I had adopted. While she already made the decision to pursue ministry full-time, meeting me, and talking with other missionaries like Ilsia and Lidia, inspired her to do more. She didn't just want to pray, give, and travel. She also wanted to support other missionaries—to adopt, love, and care for them. She later told me that working with me is what caused her to catch the larger vision of missionary work. She, too, wanted to adopt another missionary and commit herself to support them through and through. And, she did! Raphael, a young man who attended her church at the time, began asking her for advice on what it takes to follow Christ, and she led him to begin ministry at UCCR Bible Institute. In other words, Marisol listened to the urge she had to do more with missions. And, I am humbled to realize that she credited this step forward to me. Because while she had said that she wanted to do more missions like me, I was saying in my own heart that I wanted to do more missions like her!

In fact, her devotion—not just to the mission field, but to Jesus—was further proven one day while she and I were serving. I noticed that, while working, she would often toy with a ring on the ring finger of her left hand. At this point, she and I had become close friends, and she hadn't mentioned a husband. When I had asked her about it, she smiled and shook her head and began explaining to me an honorable explanation behind the ring. She had told me that the ring wasn't a sign of marriage to any man. Instead, it was a purity ring she wanted to wear for Jesus.

"I'm married to Him before I'm married to anyone else," she explained.

Her response brought tears to my eyes.

This ring made her decision to leave the academic world for the sake of winning souls for Jesus all the more significant. She left the university where she studied *and* the comfort of her home to stay at Last Harvest Master's Commission for three years. There she would carry out pastoral practices in the country and several short term missions' trips in Colombia in the year 2011, Ecuador in 2012, and Belize in 2013. She completed her basic level studies in the A/D Biblical Institution, and in her third year, she was approved as a missionary to Peru by the National Missions Department A/D El Salvador and travel for four months in Peru—defining her call to be a missionary.

Therefore, for her to say that she was inspired by me to do more missionary work blew me away because I felt just the same about her.

The irony is what connected us.

I didn't just teach Marisol; Marisol taught me.

Marisol didn't just learn from me; I learned from Marisol.

And, because the dynamic of our friendship was not a one-way exchange, our conversations would often be teary-eyed and heartfelt.

"You made me good-cry, Dad," she would say to me at times. And, her showing me a picture of her engagement ring from her fiancé, Miguel, was one of those moments.

All of those years she decided to stay pure for Jesus soon turned into her saying yes to the man God gave her to marry. Receiving the news of her engagement was a highlighted proud-father moment for me. As Marisol would put it, a "good-cry" indeed. Who knew that I would share the celebratory moment with her years later as her friend and father? Only God! He ordained our connection. And, I am certain that there are God-ordained friendships out there for you too. Chances are, they may be ready for you in places you aren't looking. As you begin to discover the corner of the world God is calling you to, consider the fact that you may have to be willing to get uncomfortable. Because, who knows? That may be the place where your next friendship lies. The Lord could have a divine connection waiting for you in your obedience. There could be a person—a place—He's assigned to you where He can grow and stretch you into the person He's called you to be as you learn. With the amount I've learned from Marisol and the amount she's claimed to learn from me, I am most thankful that I decided to attend that first missionary trip to El Salvador. Without it, I wouldn't have felt inclined to go in the year of 2010, not being able to meet her. And, what if there's a person you're supposed to meet that you won't be able to because you're saying no?

There's only one way to find out.

You're just going to have to say yes.

CHAPTER FIVE

Wendy & Gustavo

Who knew that my tiny "Yes" would result in such blessings? Knowing Marisol has enriched my life and ultimately reminded me of the necessity of missions and the sponsoring of many other missionaries, which leads me to introduce another incredible couple that I wouldn't have been able to meet if it weren't for Holy Spirit's prompting—Wendy & Gustavo.

I know this beautiful couple now to be two influential servant-hearted people. However, their story goes back to the year 2000—Wendy's story specifically. This was the year she encountered Christ, which was the most beautiful moment she's ever experienced before in her life, she said. She had many problems back home that kept her from experiencing Christ's beauty sooner. But, after participating in a devotional at the school where she studied, she heard the gospel through a preacher, who—little did he know—preached about everything Wendy was facing at the time. From the trial she was undergoing, the difficulties she was enduring, everything the preacher preached that day was exactly what she needed to say, "Yes," to Jesus. And, she did! She was fifteen when this happened. And, though it was hard for her to make it to church due to her home life, she still attended anyway and went far in her walk with the Lord.

A month after accepting Jesus into her heart, she became a part of King's Castle ministry—the same ministry the aforementioned missionaries in this book took part in as well. She grew and learned a lot during her time there and knew it was the place the Lord was calling her to when she realized she couldn't be without it. She left King's Castle at the age of twenty to study medicine at a different university, but nothing felt more at home than King's Castle did, and she returned—solidifying that that was where the Lord wanted her. She decided to join Master's Commission in the year of 2008, and it was there she was able to learn more about the Lord, living totally dependent on Him. And, just like the other missionaries mentioned, our two worlds collided, and a long-lasting connection was formed between us.

Ironically enough, I met Wendy the same year she first joined Master's Commission—2008. Our exchange was ordinary, certainly not suggestive of a long-lasting father-daughter relationship. We were working with a handful of our students from our church's school of ministry, helping to build El Salvador's own school of ministry—a bible college—by pouring nearly 40 yards of concrete down in one day's time. We only had a total of four guys and ten girls, so it was a lot of hard work. However, to motivate our labor to completion, one of the workers teased us with a trip down to the lake once the work was finished.

"¡Vengo, vengo!" the worker would say, which in Spanish meant, "Come, come!".

I didn't know that this silly little phrase made a connection between Wendy and me, especially since we had little communication, until I came back again in 2010—two years later. She smiled at me and knew by my expression that I was unsure of who she was. It wasn't until she quietly approached me with the familiar phrase, "¡Vengo, vengo!" that I remembered her from that day of work back in 2008. From that point on, we became close friends. When I learned in 2012 that she was in the same class as Marisol, I was amazed!Each student seemed to connect me with the next, and I seemed to have discovered which friendship tied to the other the more I visited. I was so excited to know that there was so much community in El Salvador, and I was and am thankful that the Lord called me to be a part of it. Pouring into Wendy as a father-figure in her life was rewarding once I learned that she did not have a great relationship with her father growing up. Who would've thought that God would call me all the way out to El Salvador to be that for her? His divine connections are amazing.

While Wendy associated with a lot of people, pastors, and missionaries through King's Castle, there was one introduction that was most important—her strong, hardworking, and compassionate husband, Gustavo.

I was able to meet Gustavo right around the time both he and Wendy were appointed as leaders of Master's Commission—the same ministry Wendy attended when I first met her in 2008. This gave me a chance to learn more about Gustavo as he was serving in this new role as leader.

However, it wasn't until the year 2014 when I began to connect most with Gustavo. After expressing to me some of his new challenges as leader, I began to give him fatherly advice.

Gustavo had told me that year what was going on behind the scenes of his new leadership position. In a few short words, he told me how he had been mistreated by his students. There was a lack of respect, very few of them complied with his directions. He was having trouble establishing authority. And, as he spoke, I was reminded of what I had learned serving in the Marines.

"We can't lead from behind," I told him. "Lead in front. We can't lead and not do what we're commanding."

After Gustavo had put this into practice, leading by example and modeling what he hoped to see in his students, he noticed a significant change in his leadership, and therefore, in his students. From that point on, he considered me as his father, and I considered him as my son. And, though it would be years before I was able to hold Wendy's and Gustavo's children—Lucas and Valentina— these early years of watching them grow in their marriage and calling reminded me of why missionary work is crucial. I was able to partner and help them not just in ministry, but in everyday life. Like kids coming to a father, they would call me when they needed help. It has always been my joy to respond with a helping hand. And, since having their son, Lucas, and their daughter, Valentina, they have become like grandchildren to me. I love to support them and watch them grow in their education. Being a part of their family in El Salvador, as well as having them be a part of my family in the states, just goes to show how big God's family is and how intentional He is about building it. He didn't just call me to be a part of a local family, but a global one as well—a family only *He* could build. And, do you want to know something, reader? You're a part of this family too. If Jesus is your Lord and Savior, you are family with believers all around the world. Wouldn't you like to meet them? And, better yet, complete missions to make more disciples? Or, in other words, brothers and sisters? Don't forget: This is what we're called to do as believers—to go out into all the world and make disciples. I'm happy to have been able to do that alongside my family. And, I can assure you that you too will find joy when you decide to go out and evangelize as well.

My relationship with Gustavo and Wendy reminds me all the more of why going out into all the world and preaching the gospel is important, as the two led to yet another introduction: Wendy's and Marisol's classmate. She's bright, compassionate, and has a burning heart for Jesus.

Her name is Vanessa.

Terri and Don Triplett with Pastor Julio & Pastor Matty & family

Vanessa & I ready to do ministry in El Salvador

Marisol & I cheesing at the camera!

Vanessa & Emily (missionary) doing ministry work

JUST SAY YES, AND GO!

Vanessa, Wendy, & I having fun in the kitchen!

Ilsia, Aracely, Kimmy, and I during a life-giving lunch break

Marisol (being herself!) with her nieces & nephews

Vanessa, geared up & ready to work!

Jocelyn & I during one of my many visits!

Pastor Julio and I, posing with his mother & children

lsia, Daniel, and I with Priyanka (their daughter) in India

Marisol and I, posing with her family

Ilsia praying at La Carpa in 2008

Marcela and her mother in Romania

Vanessa & Dr. Boris geared up for ministry

Pastor Juan Rivera, Marcela, & Efron at Victory Church

Gustavo, Wendy, and I with their 2 children (who I consider my grandkids!)

Terri & Don Triplett with Lidia during a missions' trip!

Vanessa and I with her family

Pastor Julio and Pastor Matty with their children

Gustavo ordaining Terri & Don Triplett's
vow renewal ceremony

CHAPTER SIX

VANESSA

Here is the question I will continue to ask as you
read through the pages of this book:

What if God wants to use you outside of your comfort zone?

What if there's someone in a different part of what you consider to be "your world" in need?

What if they are waiting for you to say, "Yes," because you're the one God wants to use to bless them?

My trips to El Salvador are a testament of what God can do through the doorway of obedience. Vanessa's story is more proof. Coming from her directly, she shares her testimony of how someone else's obedience can be another person's blessings. Read her words, and consider the many other miracle stories others could be writing if you would just follow the urge of Holy Spirit.

This is her story:

It was in 2010. I remember I was merged in full-time training to become a missionary. I always served God with all my heart and that year was a year full of blessings. I marked dates of weeks that I wanted to always remain in my memory and would never forget. In March of that year, we received teams of people from the United States of America to work on street evangelism. A team from Ohio called Victory—which everyone mentioned was very special— came and in my heart, I asked God in prayer to work with them.

A few weeks later, God answered my prayer by granting me to work with them. Victory was a very special team indeed. That week, I met wonderful people with whom I still keep in touch. I met this wonderful lady—her name is Susan—with whom I became friends with. After twelve years, we still talk. We hope one day to see each other. "If not on earth, then we will meet in heaven," is what she would always tell me. We have a beautiful friendship and always support each other in prayer.

I remember Susan was the friend with whom I managed to make a special connection from the Victory team that year. Eddie was also on the team, but we didn't find that opportunity to get connected as friends on that occasion. One never knows the paths that God will use to connect people. Years later in 2016, while posting on my Facebook wall, suddenly a photo of my friend Wendy appeared. Underneath that photo, Eddie made a comment encouraging her to speak English. I responded that she only sang in English (which she did jokingly). It was through that post that Eddie and I got connected. Soon after that exchange of comments, he sent me a message asking how I knew Wendy and if I spoke English. I answered yes. Wendy is one of my best friends. During that time, I spoke a little English since it is a language that I have always been passionate about since my childhood.

From that moment forward, Eddie and I began to share experiences of missions' trips. He shared with me how during all his travels, God placed spiritual sons and daughters in his life so that he could help them on the faith journey that many of us were going through. We talked for months. When I was about to graduate from nursing school, I uploaded a photo on Facebook of my last day of social service in the hospital. Eddie messaged me and asked if it would soon be my graduation. At that time, I was not sure of graduating since I had to pay a lot of money, money that I did not have. He asked me the reason for this situation, to which I was honest. He immediately replied that he would help me. This was a response from God for me. In my mind, I began to reflect, and I said to myself:

"If God brought me to this place, He would be the one who would provide for my graduation."

I made a plan to ask some of my relatives for help and to also work as hard as I could to make some money to achieve my goal. Weeks later, Eddie sent a message and told me that he had already deposited all of my graduation money! I burst into tears, tears of joy coming out of my eyes, as no one had ever done anything like this for me in my life! I was the first in my class to pay all of the graduation fees— something that had never happened before. But my God, who knows the desires of our hearts, was faithful in providing everything I needed.

I managed to graduate that year, and after a while, I continued serving God full-time with my career, living only by faith. When the COVID-19 pandemic began, God put it in my heart to serve on the front line. He gave me a VIP pass so I could enter a hospital where only health personnel were allowed. During that time, God allowed me to guide souls towards Him in their last breath of life. All of this happened thanks to someone who believed in me and in the call that God had given me throughout my career. Eddie has been more than a blessing for my life and for my family. He is the spiritual father that God chose to help me on this difficult path called life. He has helped me make very important decisions. In 2021, God took my biological father, but we know that He never leaves us alone and helpless. God puts special people who help us in the most difficult moments of our lives. Eddie has been one of those people for me. That is why I honor my Christ for putting such a special person in my path. Words are not enough to thank how good God is.

Who knew that one single comment on Facebook would lead to souls won for Jesus? Vanessa's story reminds me that God doesn't waste anything. A comment led to a graduation gift. A graduation gift led to people giving their heart to Christ as they took their last breath. How God uses each step of obedience is extraordinarily humbling. Not to mention, the way God works makes me all the more eager to obey, even if it might not make sense. You never know which person, place, or connection God will use for His divine story. You never know what He might do. But, just as Vanessa saw for herself working in a hospital—and just as we all see every single day—there are so many lost souls that need to be found. There are so many people who still need the Lord. The call to go out and make disciples isn't for the next believer. It's for you. It's time to stop fighting back against the urge and just say yes.

CHAPTER SEVEN

JOCELYN

Revelation 12:11 NIV says this:
"They triumphed over him by the blood of the Lamb and by the word of their testimony…"

If there's anything I've learned as a missionary (and, what I hope you've been learning as you read through this book), is that testimonies are powerful. They have the power to relate to a non-believer and pull them into your world of faith. It's a way to get to know someone better, and ultimately, a way to see another unique dimension of how Jesus works. At least that's how I felt hearing Jocelyn's testimony—another dynamic and influential missionary I'm excited to introduce you to. I met Jocelyn in the year of 2014 and worked alongside her in different areas of the ministry. What started off as an invitation to get ice cream after a long day of work turned into another chance to meet more of God's family. I asked Jocelyn for her testimony and what she told me has stuck with me since.

She didn't have to go too far into her story before I realized how smart she was. She was incredibly intelligent. The fact that she aspired to be a doctor didn't shock me at all. What did shock me, however, was how sad and traumatic her childhood was. She didn't have the best relationship with her mother growing up. From abandonment to verbal abuse, Jocelyn wasn't close with her and instead lived with her father and grandmother. Thankfully, years after Jocelyn and I had formed a bond by working together, I was able to meet her father.

We both agree that this was our favorite memory.

I loved meeting her father because Jocelyn had already become like a daughter to me at that point. Therefore, to have the privilege of meeting her biological dad was indescribable, as I was able to learn more about their family history. But, the reason why our meeting was Jocelyn's favorite memory was because she discovered something she had been missing her entire life, something that I didn't even realize how big of a deal it was until she called it out. During the time I was mentoring Jocelyn, I would tell her often how proud of her I was. Through constant encouragement, support, and a helping hand, I would frequently remind her of how brilliant of a worker she is and that her faith shone as bright as the sun. Jocelyn didn't realize how much she needed to hear those words not just from me, but from her biological father. And, after having the privilege of telling her biological father directly how proud I was of her, he began to use that same language with Jocelyn—language she hadn't heard from him before. To have those words come from him meant the world to her. It was what she needed to heal and to keep working hard, doing what God called her to do.

Jocelyn today is still serving and working hard, going to church and supporting her family still in El Salvador. With family members connected to Ilsia's family, I couldn't be more proud of how the two of them work so hard to advance the kingdom. And, while I wasn't aware of how impactful my words to her would be and what my role as a father figure in her life would play, God knew. And, God cared enough about Jocelyn to make sure she heard those words from her father, even if He had to go to the extent of sending someone from a different country to initiate the moment. So, what began as a missions' trip to get Nancy Ashman off my back resulted in a young El Salvadorian girl getting an emotional need met because her heavenly Father knew she needed it. Therefore, I will continue Nancy's legacy—constantly urging others around me to pursue the call He gave to every believer in Mark 16:15. Saying, "Yes," may look different for everyone, but everyone's, "Yes," gives glory to the same God. I've seen the benefits of responding. Now, it's your turn to see for yourself too.

CHAPTER EIGHT

Pastor Matty

One of the most prominent quotes Jesus gave us
during His time here on earth is found in Matthew 16:18 NIV:

"And I tell you that you are Peter, and on this rock I will build my church, and the gates of Hades will not overcome it."

This is the Scripture where Jesus assures us that He is the one building the church—His body. And, part of the experience of going out into the world to evangelize means you get to meet many of those who represent the church too. Some people won't be in full-time ministry, and others will—many like the missionaries I've mentioned in this book so far. And, so it is the case for the next two ministers featured in this chapter: Pastors Matty and Julio.

Both have incredible testimonies. Both of their stories are woven with the goodness and miraculous power of God. As their marriage has blessed not only my life, but the lives of those they touched in El Salvador, I'm excited to share just a piece of what God has done through them in building His church. Matty's testimony is as follows:

When Matty was little, she had a very difficult childhood. She suffered from poverty, abuse, and the divorce of her parents, causing her to grow up with a lot of hatred towards them. She lived in many houses with different families until she was adopted by one of her aunts. The aunt who adopted her enrolled her in a school called Liceo Cristiano Juan Bueno. Meeting a group of young people from King's Castle that worked with this schoolis how she met God. She began to serve God in her youth and attended Victory Christian Center, which was a church that supported the school she went to through Assemblies of God. Her life began to change the more she attended church and especially when she met Julio.

Matty and Julio got married in 1995. In 1996, their first son was born. Their second son came in 1999, and in 2002, their last child—a daughter—was born. Matty became a secretary and also began a career in cosmetology. She had two beauty salons, which were quite successful. Yet, she was still able to serve in King's Castle. However, in the year 2010, God called her and Julio to the pastoral ministry, which revealed what Matty wanted to do all along. She knew she and her family were called to serve God full-time in ministry. So, in December of 2010, Matty left all of her work behind in the beauty business, and she and Julio moved their whole family to a place called Potrerillos to serve God. She began to work with the women of that place through cosmetology and sewing workshops, which was highly influential in their region.

Yet, when the year 2013 rolled around, a tragedy occurred. Matty was diagnosed with breast cancer. Their family had no choice but to return to San Salvador for her health. But, thankfully, God performed a miracle and healed her! Their family returned to Potrerillos the following year in 2014.

However, the year after in 2015, the cancer came back.

And, this time, it was worse.

Her cancer was visible in her abdomen and ferociously invaded all of her organs. This second diagnosis didn't cause them to move back home, however. This time, they decided to stay in Potrerillos and continue serving God.

At the end of the year 2016, God worked a miracle.

It went like this:

As the cancer in Matty's body made her extremely ill, her family watched her breathing stop in the house where she was staying, and she was pronounced dead. And, just as the family was all ready to mourn—just as their hearts were being burdened with sadness—in an instant, her body experienced a miraculous resurrection. God brought her back to life! After this, the doctors did many tests and declared her free of cancer!

We celebrated.

We cheered.

Matty spread the word like wildfire about what God did in her life, sharing her testimony wherever God allowed her to go. And, He was glorified for all of those three years Matty testified about the miracle that had taken place in her body. But, when those three years ended, God's plans for her began to look differently than we planned.

The last place she went to minister was in Ecuador, where God used her life to perform miracles and wonders. Yet, on October 8th, 2019, God called her home to be with Him forever.

The legacy she left behind was incredible.

To this day, many people fondly and lovingly remember her. Their lives were impacted through her complete dedication to the Lord. Even since her passing, people still share how influenced they've been by the legacy she left behind.

I share this story with you to ask you a very important question:

What legacy are *you* leaving behind?

God allotted a specific time for Pastor Matty to live out the call on her life. I'm writing this to you as a reminder that He's allotted a specific time for you too. What will you do with it? Where are you going to take it? Who do you want to impact? What words do you still want to ring true long after the Lord calls you home?

Now is a good time to ask both yourself and the Lord. Matty never missed an opportunity to preach the good news. Even as she thrived as a business woman, she put the Lord in the very center of her success. How can you glorify God in the things you put your hand to? How can you make the Lord known in the short time He's assigned to you? Ask the Holy Spirit. Jot down His response here:

_____

_____

_____

_____

_____

_____

_____

_____

_____

_____

_____

Her husband, Pastor Julio, as well as their three children (David—missionary to Bolivia, Kevin—still involved in church, and Katie—finalizing her degree inmultimedia), and I, still keep in touch today. They are like family to my wife and me, as well as to our church family. God is still using Julio to build His church, and he hasn't stopped carrying on Matty's legacy. She lives on through the promise of her favorite Scripture, a promise that brings comfort to those planning to go out into all the world:

"For I know the plans I have for you," declares the Lord, *"plans to prosper you and not to harm you, plans to give you hope and a future."* — Jeremiah 29:11 NIV

CHAPTER NINE

MADELINE

As Jeremiah 29:11 served as Pastor Matty's favorite verse, the depth of that Scripture goes deeper than most people realize. In that verse, God was talking to the Israelites, His people who were currently in captivity. While He spoke good plans over them, they were still held captive.

Sometimes, following the call on your life may come with difficulties. There may be moments where you feel imprisoned or bound or held captive, even as you work with a servant's heart. But, just as God spoke a good plan and promise over those in captivity back then, we can trust that He's also speaking those things to us now. In other words, we can trust that in everything we walk through, we can always find a purpose for it. God doesn't waste a thing, even the most painful of pasts. And, if there's anyone who can testify about this, it would be a team leader who I had the privilege of meeting on my most recent trip to El Salvador. Her name is Madeline, for whom I have a special place in my heart.

Madeline is a young girl who looks a lot like my biological niece. Therefore, I always considered her to be like family. I couldn't help but to ask for her testimony once I learned that she would be our team lead and translator for our 2020 trip. What she shared was encouraging. Not to mention, a perfect reminder that God injects purpose in everything we do, promising that His plans for us are prosperous and good.

Madeline's story proves it, and she shares it with us here:

I grew up with an aunt until I was nine. My father went to prison when I was five. I have 11 siblings, all from different moms. One of my oldest sisters came to visit us, and she decided to take us from my aunt because her husband was a drunkard. Being separated from my aunt was hard because she was most like a mom to me. When my father came out of jail, he and my stepmother started to take care of my brother and me.

During three years, everything was almost good. But then, my father started to have more women in his life, and he also started to consume alcohol. He got violent and used to hurt my stepmother and me. If our family had a tragedy occur or if trouble came our way, I would feel guilty because of that. Eventually, my father said that he didn't want to have my brother and me in his house. One of my older sisters called my mom and told her we were in trouble, telling her that she needed to take care of us as a result.

She came for a month to El Salvador in 2007 when I was fifteen years old. She brought me to church. It was not my desire to go with her, but the Lord was talking to me. On one of those Sundays when we attended, the pastor made a call. I wasn't really paying attention to what he was preaching, but something inside of me was burning. After a while, I decided to come to the altar. When I came out from my seat, I started to cry. I didn't know why I was crying.

When I started to repeat the salvation prayer, I cried more, but was confused at the beginning. It was not because of sadness, or anger, but I felt so loved for the first time.

Ten years have passed since that day, and the reminder of God's love still keeps me strong.

Five years ago, I started a process in UCCR (Última Cosecha Castillo del Rey)—a missionary school. I have been prepared, and now, I am a missionary in Ecuador. I am sure it is just the beginning, but during all these years, the Lord has shown His mercy, and His love for me. It is too much to say, but, I just want to tell you, there is a purpose for your life, as it was in mine.

What better person to remind you that you have a purpose than Madeline? After all that she's walked through, we can trust her when she says God uses all things for our good, for the good of those who love Him and are called according to His purpose, as said in Romans 8:28. And, in the same way He showed her, God is willing to show you too. Ask God what that purpose for your life is and trust that He'll reveal it to you.

CHAPTER TEN

JENNIFER

Jeremiah 1:5 NIV says, "Before I formed you in the womb I knew you, before you were born I set you apart; I appointed you as a prophet to the nations."

This means that while a lot of us spend our lives wondering what God's purpose is for us, God already had it figured out long ago—before we were even formed in our mother's wombs, He promises. Therefore, we don't have to worry about where God might take us, because while it might be a mystery to us, it certainly isn't a mystery to Him. But, in case you feel as if you are alone in your searching, desperately wanting to know what God might have in store for you, I want to introduce you to another missionary I met following the call on my life.

Her name is Jennifer.

I first met Jennifer in the year 2022. At first glance, I thought she was a teenager, which was why I was so impressed with her work ethic because she was so young. However, by the first introduction, I learned that I was wrong. She wasn't a teenager; she was thirty! Not only that, but she came from a prestigious background, earning the title of Lawyer and Notary of the Republic of El Salvador in 2018 after graduating from her university.

But, even though she earned this title, life looked different for her moving forward. The closer we got, the more I got to learn about it.

Her testimony ministered to me greatly.

I learned that she met Jesus in the year 2011 at the age of twenty. She credits it as the best day of her life, as the Lord broke all of her chains. Therefore, she longed to serve Him, asking Him to use her life to preach the gospel to the masses, spreading His love and His truth. However, in the year 2012, her pastor at that time delivered to her a discouraging, and sadly, untrue message that broke her heart. She was told that she wouldn't be able to pursue full-time ministry because she was a woman, and women couldn't do that.

This hurt her deeply, as she felt so sure that this was something God had called her to do. And, when she had shared with me the pain of that moment, I knew exactly what I had to do:

Encourage her.

I quoted Jeremiah 1:5 to her, explaining that there was nothing on earth that could stop the plan God had before the very beginning of time. If God called her to it, then it's her assignment to carry out. No one was going to be able to stop her from pursuing that dream. And, it was in that moment of encouragement when I became grateful that God used my small act of obedience to come alongside her in a time of need—how He would allow me the opportunity to use His word to lift her up and not tear her down, to provide the truth to defeat the lie she received from others.

This is a crucial part of missionary work. It's a lot more than giving money. Missionary work is also prayer and encouragement, being there for people when they need you. And, I believe the mission field is ripe with Jennifers who need the church's encouragement, people who need to be championed and provided the truth of God's word instead of their own traditionalized opinion. There are some Jennifers out there only I can encourage, and others that only you can encourage. Will you? They are waiting for you to say yes.

It was heart-warming for me to see how my encouragement moved her along. As painful as it was to hear the words of her previous pastor, she continued to push through and soon found herself working with the Assemblies of God Ministry in Castillo del Rey in 2020. It was here she discovered that God had a purpose for her life and that He does, in fact, want to use her for ministry work. When she learned this, she constantly asked the Lord, "Show me what You've called me to. Show me what You've called me to." God answered her faithfully and clearly in the year 2021. He confirmed the call to go to the mission field.

She didn't hesitate.

Right away, she entered into the UCCR Last Harvest King's Castle program, not wanting to let any more time pass. She was thirty years old when she received that call from God. And, for a while, her age discouraged her.

For months, she would ask God, "Why did I discover my call so late? Why did I have to wait until this age for me to understand what I was called to and not when I was younger, like how others around me discovered it?"

She had felt that she had wasted time in her youth and cried many tears over what she had been calling a delay. Yet, her grief is what made her all the more passionate to follow the Lord, going into ministry full-time.

In making this decision, she left a lot of familiar zones behind, including her profession. She earned a bachelor's degree in Legal Sciences in 2014, which led her to her career as lawyer in 2018. But, she felt the call to ministry so strongly that she left that world for the mission field. She entered the university without God, but she graduated with Him, and she counts it pure joy that God didn't give her a job in the Supreme Court of Justice, the job she had planned for.

"My dream is God's dream," she said. "I want to go to the nations and talk about Jesus with those who need Him."

While Jennifer has decided this for herself, here is the question:

What about you?

Is your dream God's dream? Because if it is His dream, there is absolutely nothing that can stop you. You don't have to fear going into the corner of the world He's called you to because He already has a purpose and plan for you to be there. Just like Jennifer learned, people can't disqualify you if God's called you to do something.

Not even you can.

Maybe you're reading this, and you've disqualified yourself from what He's called you to. Or, you're discouraged because someone told you you couldn't do it either. In the same way I encouraged Jennifer with Jeremiah 1:5, I want to encourage you as well. He has always had a purpose for you, a good and pleasing will for your life. No one can stop it if God's already assigned you to it before the world even began. Don't give up on following His plan just because someone else doesn't agree or understand. Stay faithful to His command. You're not too young or too old. You're exactly the kind of person God wants to use. So, let Him use you. Just say yes. And, He will show you where to go.

EPILOGUE

This is certainly not the end of the story. After serving as a missionary to El Salvador for twenty years, the stories written in this book barely even scratch the surface. There are still so many names I could write about, so many stories I could record. One book alone wouldn't be able to contain all of them at once. However, while the stories are endless, the message in each of them is clear:

One *yes* can produce more than you realize. And, God wants to use your life to win souls for the Kingdom.

Ministry, in any capacity, is always full-time. Even as a part-time missionary, you can still complete full-time ministry.

Do you want to know how?

It's because there is no distance in prayer. You may not always be with the people you're called to, but you can always pray for them. Distance does not affect the power of prayer. I've learned as an American missionary to El Salvador—a country thousands of miles away from my home—I may not be with them in flesh, but I'm certainly with them in spirit. And, they're with me too—encouraging me and praying for me. I could not be more grateful. As much joy as I have in going out into the world God's assigned for me, I want you to experience that same joy. Look at all of what God could do through one act of obedience. As uncomfortable, challenging, and unclear as it may feel, allow these stories to remind you that the call is worth it.

Saying yes is worth it. Spreading the gospel is worth it. And, just like I had no idea that so many stories would come from my small act of obedience, you also won't be able to imagine what God will do through your obedience too.

JUST SAY YES, AND GO!

ABOUT THE AUTHOR

Edward Rudolphi is a missionary, husband, father, friend, and most importantly, a follower of Jesus Christ. Ed was moved to document his journeys after being persuaded to join the mission field twenty years after he said, "Yes." He decided to write about his experiences and persuade others to hopefully just say yes, and go! He plans to record more of his journeys in upcoming books and other projects as well.

One-hundred-percent of the proceeds will go to the missionaries written about in the book to help assist them as they continue their ministry wherever God calls them.

Made in the USA
Monee, IL
21 September 2023

43135241R00059